Who Could Love You More Than Me?

BY

Cassity Riffe McCool-Solis

ILLUSTRATED BY

Reagan S. Weedman

To Noah Scott, you are my whole heart. You put value to these words. Who could love you more than me?

With special thanks to Drew, the way you believe in me is magical.

Little One, there may come a day when you will wonder how much I love you.

When that day comes, I'll ask you to think, "Who could love you more than me?"

Just ask the wind as she tickles the trees, but she'll never know

who could love you more than me.

You could search the great big universe and the whole deep blue sea,

but never find anyone who could love you more than me!

Climb the highest mountain and search from its peak,

but still you won't see anyone

who could love you more than me.

Sneak through the forest, ask the creatures that you see,

from the majestic owl to the buzzing bee.

"WHOOOOOOOO, WHOOO, Who could love you more than me?"

You can travel this great nation!

From Texas to Kentucky, and still you'll wonder

who could love you more than me.

Look the whole world over! Ask anyone you meet!

And still no one, not one, could love you more than me.

Ask the moon and read all the stars in the whole galaxy,

but they won't know who could love you more than me.

Sit quietly and consider all life's beauty.

You'll know lots more,

but not who could love you more than me.

I'll sing it from the rooftops and into every valley.

"I love you! I love you!"

So who could love you more than me?

Little One, you are fiercely loved and cherished abundantly.

Who could love you more than me?

And each night, as you drift off to sleep,

I whisper, "Thank You, Jesus."

Because He is the only One who could love you more than me.

"Give thanks to the God of heaven.
His love endures forever."

Psalm 136:26

Made in the USA
Lexington, KY
23 April 2018